A SMACK IN THE PUS

Also by Scott Simpson

SHUT YER PUS

A SMACK
IN THE PUS

SCOTTISH STREET ETIQUETTE FOR BEGINNERS

SCOTT SIMPSON

BLACK & WHITE PUBLISHING

First published 2005
by Black & White Publishing Ltd
99 Giles Street, Edinburgh EH6 6BZ

ISBN 1 84502 066 9

Text and illustrations copyright © Scott Simpson 2005

British Library Cataloguing in Publication Data:
A catalogue record for this book is available
from the British Library.

Cover illustration by
Scott Simpson & Joni Hawley

Printed and bound by Nørhaven Paperback A/S

CONTENTS

A great big fat thanks to Shona for being my best pal. To Dean, Joanne, Kirsty and Leigh for making me smile, Emma for making Dean smile and young Craig for making everyone smile at a reasonable price.

Thanks must also go to Billy (The Pig) Owens for going above and beyond the call of duty.

Cheers to John and Anna at Lomond and to Campbell, Alison and everyone at Black & White Publishing.

Finally, I'd like to say a huge thank you to Joni Hawley who put so much time and effort into this book. 'Ah couldnae huv done it withoot ye!'

SS

This book is dedicated to Spider
1987-2005

INTRODUCTION

Worried about numpties, bammers and doughheids? Not sure about how deal with knife-wielding maniacs, beggars, drunks, choobs, neds and bampots? Well, just in case you get into any tricky situations on the streets of Scotland, *A Smack in the Pus* will help keep you right on the unwritten rules of the street and hopefully help you avoid getting a smack in the pus. And as with street etiquette the world over, the smallest things can start a swedge if you don't know the unwritten rules of the street, so keep the heid.

1

MEETING AND GREETING

When meeting someone for the first time it is customary to shake hands. Scots rarely kiss or embrace strangers unless they are drunk, in which case they all but hump your leg. The most common greeting in Scotland is **Hiya,** which you can follow up with any of the following useful phrases:

Howzitgaun?
How are things going?

How ye dae'in?
How are you doing?

Yupty?
What have you been doing with yourself lately?

Ah've no seen ye fur yonks.
It's been quite some time since last we met.

Should the person you are talking to turn out to be

3

tedious company you can always excuse yourself with the following phrases.

Ah better git gaun.
I must be going.

Ah better shoot the craw, the wife'll be dae'in ur dinger.
I really must get going, my wife will be wondering where I've got to.

Geez a bell sometime.
We must keep in touch.

When it comes to bidding a fond farewell, the Scots like to keep things as brief as possible.

Tro.
Cheerio.

2

INSULTS AND SWEARING

Once you're past the meeting and greeting stage things get a bit trickier and if there's one thing the Scots excel at it's pointing out the shortcomings of others. Be they unnecessarily talkative, sexually unattractive or just plain stupid, the Scots have a word for them. This list is far from exhaustive but here are just a few examples.

The following words, which for some mysterious reason all begin with D, are used to illustrate the incompetence of those nearest and dearest to you.

Ding-ul, dipstick, dooboo, dumplin, doughheid

For example a mother might enquire of her children:

Which wan o' you dumplins traipsed shite aw oo'er ma doonstairs cairpit?
Which of you young scallywags has trodden dog dirt all over the downstairs rug?

The next batch of insults, many of which are slang

5

expressions used to describe male and female genitalia, are reserved for those who warrant a sterner reprimand.

pie, prick, numpty, pleb, fanny, erse, dick-heid, dobber, nob, walloper, doss-cunt, baw-bag, cunty-baws, dick, trumpet, mad-rocket, galloot, glaikit-basturt

Haw fanny-baws, gonnae keep the rammy doon?
Excuse me you inconsiderate oaf, but would you mind keeping the noise to a minimum?

The following insults are more commonly aimed at a specific type of person. Those who avoid any form of violent physical contact can be described as **poofs, saps, jessies** and **big fearties**.

Wee Alec took pelters oaf eh's pals whin he shat it fae a pagger wi Shuggie. Mind you, wee Alec's no goat is minny mars bars is Shuggy.
Young Alexander took no amount of ridicule from his friends when he backed out of a fight with Hugh. There again, it has to be said that young Alexander has had far fewer facial wounds than Hugh.

Those who are capable of talking the hind legs of a **cuddy** (donkey) are sometimes referred to as a **blether, haiver, gibber, spraff** or one who simply **talks pish**.

You dinnae hauf spout a load o' shite whin yer peeved.
You do have an awful habit of talking nonsense when you've been drinking.

There are a number of colourful expressions one can use when describing the appearance of someone who has taken a **heider** (tumble) from the ugly tree and hit every branch on the way down.

A face like a burst couch.
A face like a squashed tomata.
A face like a well skelped erse.
A face like a blind cobbler's thumb.

Dinnae git eh's wrong, Tam's a barry gadgie, bit eh's goat a coupon like a bulldug lickin pish oaf a nettle.
Whereas I have nothing but respect and admiration for Thomas, it has to be said that he's not the most handsome of God's creations.

Sycophants, like the weakling who travels in the slipstream of the school bully for his own protection, are often referred to as **choobs, erselickers** or **crawlin, broon-nosed basturts**.

If Mikey gits eh's tongue any further up Drew's jeer eh could lick the back o' eh's throat.
Michael is anything but discreet when it comes to massaging Andrew's ego.

There is a certain type of person who, had it not been for a Conservative government policy of releasing the criminally insane into the care of the community, would still be safely tucked up in a big soft room wearing pyjamas which button up the back.

These potentially homicidal individuals may be described as **bams, bammers, nutters, heidbangers, pure mad mental** or **total and utter cycle paths.**

Ah widnae go nippin Norrie's heid when eh's been on the cheeky watter if ah wis you cos eh's goat an awfy habit o' gaun radge n' glessin folk.
If I were you I would avoid antagonising Norman when he has quite clearly had too much to drink as he has a quick temper and has been known to lash out.

The male bias in Scot's slang is best exemplified in the fact that the number of expressions used to describe sexually liberated women vastly outnumber those used to describe their male counterparts.

There are probably only two expressions for a young chap with a great many notches on his bedpost, which are **shagger** and **hoor-maister.** More often than not these are both given and taken as compliments.

Women get, for want of a better phrase, the shitty end of this particular stick.

Upon losing their virginity females find themselves tarred with a considerably wider brush. **Ride, dog, boot, cow, slag, hing-oot, brass nail, shelter-belter, root** and **gey fond o' the auld Nairobi** are all phrases used to describe a girl with a real or imagined sexual history.

Even their reproductive organs don't escape ridicule. Following numerous sexual encounters with well endowed gentlemen the poor lass might be described as having **a fanny like a welly toap, a clown's poackit, a wizard's sleeve** or other roomy object. Sexual intercourse might be likened to **hoying a sausage doon the Clyde tunnel** or **chuckin a dowt up a close.** It may become necessary **tae tie a plank tae yer erse tae stoap yersel fae fawin in.**

While on the subject of carnal desires there are myriad expressions to describe those with more exotic tastes. This could mean anything from a ménages à trois to keeping the bedroom light on.

Stealing women's undergarments from washing lines in the dead of night is known as **plamphin** or **snowdroppin.**

A purveyor of left-handed literature, also known as **scuddy books**, is a **clatty** or **clarty basturt.**

Those who partake in group sex, mild S&M, and role playing are just **queer-hawks**.

This next section deals with words which, if used in the presence of a grandparent, would have them reaching for the carbolic soap and leave you farting bubbles for a fortnight. Swearing might not be big or clever but it is an integral part of Scot's slang, the most common word being **fuck**. It can be used to express dismissal in the following ways – **fuck off, git tae fuck, git the fuck oot o' there** and **fuck this for a gemme o' soajirs.**

It can be used to describe the state of something in disrepair as in **ma motur's fucked** or someone in a state of exhaustion as in **ah'm fucked hoofin it up thae stairs.**

It can also be used as an exclamation of anger, such as, **Fuck! Ah forgot tae tape the fitba'** or surprise as in **Fuck me, ah didnae expect that!** and sometimes even contentment – **fuck me, that soup wis nice.**

In spite of its most obvious connotations the word is rarely, if ever, used in the context of sexual intercourse. Scots prefer to use **ride, cowp, shag, podger, gettin yer end away, gettin yer nazzles, John O' Groats, Cameron Toll** or **Nat King Cole.**

The word bastard is another common profanity although the Scots pronounce it **basturt**.

It can also be used to refer to a situation which has caused you some distress or displeasure.

That wuz a basturt o' a joab.

The last sweary word you need to know about is cunt. Considered by many to be the ultimate insult, this can be used in Scotland to describe those who both please and displease you, for example **some cunt's slashed the tyres oan ma motor** or **Davy's a sound cunt, eh's eyewiz goat bevvy in the fridge.** It can even be used when referring to oneself, as in **Am ah the only cunt thit's workin here?** And you probably are.

3

NEEBURS

We've all got them, we all need to deal with them and as the song says, everybody needs good neighbours. But what is a good neighbour? Perhaps they're the quiet sort who you rarely see but always receive a Christmas card from. Or someone who feeds your cat and waters the plants when you go away on holiday. Maybe they're someone with whom you can enjoy the odd chin-wag over the garden fence or someone who nips around every so often to borrow a cup of sugar. Or the not-so-good neighbour whose 400 watt stereo keeps you awake until 4 am even though you have to be up in a couple of hours to go to work. Or the one whose constant shouting and bawling habitually disturbs your quiet time on the cludgy. So as the song does indeed say, 'Everybody needs good neighbours'.

However, if we are perfectly honest with ourselves we'd probably much rather construct a ten foot deep crocodile infested moat around our homes just to keep the buggers at bay. So here's a few phrases and expressions that might come in handy when dealing with the people in your neighbourhood.

Ah see the folk fae nixt door ur flittin.
I understand that our next door neighbours are moving away.

Ah hope tae hell we dinnae git an ASBO faimly movin in.
I do hope that our new neighbours will not cause too much trouble.

Wait till ye git a deek at the faimly thits movin in nixt door.
I think you ought to come and have a look at our new next door neighbours.

If you are unfortunate enough to have a family from hell or, as they are now more commonly known, ASBOs, move into the house next door you can expect them to immediately begin taking advantage of your good nature.

Awright gadgie. We've jist moved in nixt door 'n' oor phones no gittin pit in till nixt week. Any chance ah could git a wee shot o' yours so a kin gie aw ma mates a bell n' git thum roond fur a hoose-warmin pairty. Yer welcome tae nip roond yersel bit mind 'n' bring a cargo wi ye.
Hello. My family and I have just moved in next door and as yet our phone is not connected. I was wondering if you would allow me to make a call from your phone as I have a small gathering of friends and family to arrange. You are of course welcome to attend

14

so long as you remember to supply your own refreshments.

Ah couldnae tap a boatle o' mulk till ah git ma green biro, could ah?
Could I be so bold as to borrow a bottle of milk which I shall return as soon as my unemployment benefit cheque arrives.

No doubt the day will come when you have to go and knock on their door and these phrases should help to establish a common rapport.

Dae ye want tae turn that rammy doon a bit?
Could you keep the noise down?

Wid ye tell yer bairns no tae boot thur baw against ma front door.
Would you ask your children to refrain from kicking their football against my front door.

Wid ye tell yer bairns tae stoap hoyin thur shite intae ma gairdin.
Would you ask your children to stop throwing litter into my garden.

Wid ye tell yer bairns tae stoap stickin bangers up ma cat's hole.
Would you ask your children to refrain from maiming my pet with fireworks.

Is it no aboot time ye goat aw that brock shifted oot'ay the back green?

Don't you think it's time you asked the cleansing department to remove the build up of urine stained mattresses, faulty white kitchen appliances and assorted engine parts from the communal drying area?

This basic knowledge of how to deal with your neigh-bours should help to stop open warfare in your area. Unless they're total bammers.

4

THE WEATHER

If there's one topic of conversation you'll need to be familiar with when you're out and about in Scotland, it's the weather. There is a popular misconception that visitors to Scotland can experience four seasons in one day. This is in fact utter bollocks and, if the truth be told, visitors can expect to experience four degrees of winter in one day. In fact, records show that Scotland achieved its highest ever temperature between 1.08pm and 3.47pm on the 19th August 1976 when the baking heat soared to just over nine degrees Celsius. Five million Scots proceeded to remove their coats, ice cream suddenly became more expensive than cocaine and there were two empty beds in the hypothermia ward at Aberdeen Infirmary.

Visitors to Scotland should pack plenty of jumpers, gloves, scarves, woolly hats and some sort of waterproof clothing, ideally a scuba diving suit. If you're planning to climb any of the mountains in the Highlands, don't forget to wear a T-shirt and a sturdy pair of flip-flops as this gives the mountain rescue service something to giggle at while they chip your frozen blue carcass off the side of the hill.

Here are a few handy phrases that will help you understand the weather in Scotland.

Jesus sufferin fuck, it's baltic oot thair.
Goodness me, it's rather cold outside.

It's lookin gey dreich.
It looks as though it may rain.

It's beltin doon.
It is raining.

It's bouncin doon.
It is raining.

It's bucketin doon.
It is raining.

It's chuckin it doon.
It is raining.

It's fair comin doon.
It is raining.

It's hammerin doon.
It is raining.

It's honkin doon.
It is raining.

It's hoyin doon.
It is raining.

It's lanterin doon.
It is raining.

It's peltin doon.
It is raining.

It's pishin doon.
It is raining.

It's stoatin doon.
It is raining.

And despite global warming, that's really all you'll need to know about the weather. But, if you do see the big yellow light in the sky, don't forget to take your top off as fast as possible, no matter what the temperature is, and get the Trex out to make the most of it. Unless you've just had your spray tan topped up.

5

TELLY

Telly is what gets most of us through the day and is an invaluable companion when the rain's stoatin down. Much of what's on telly may be an endless stream of pish but it's important to make sure you're watching the right pish on the right dish. Otherwise, what would you talk to your friends about apart from the weather? Here's a typical telly schedule.

SKYE WAN

9am   **NEWS AND WHAIR IT'S PISHIN DOON**

9.30am   **HOW CLARTY IS YER HOOSE?**
This week the ladies pay a visit to a man whose wife shot the craw only three days ago to find the entire hoose under five inches of stoor and the cludgy honking o' pish.

10am   **THE MAGS HAINEY SHOW**
Early mornin chat show hosted by Big Mags Hainey in which neds and Sengas settle their petty differences by screaming obscenities and attacking each other with furniture for the amusement of the viewing public. This morning's episode is entitled "Whair's ma fuckin hoosekeepin money disappeared tae?"

10.45am   **BACK WINDAE** *(film)*
Re-make of the classic Hitchcock thriller in which a stookied journalist suspects a neebur of giving his wife the severe malky. Starring Robert Carlyle, Dorothy Paul and Wee Jimmy Krankie.

21

12.30pm	**DINNERTIME NEWS AND WHAIR IT'S PISHIN DOON**

12.30pm   **DINNERTIME NEWS AND WHAIR IT'S PISHIN DOON**

1pm   **NEEBURS**
Soap opera set in the village of Kinghorn in Fife. This week Archie accuses Morag of being in league with Lucifer and has her burned at the stake.

1.30pm   **CANNAE COOK, WULLNAE COOK**
This week Nick fae Nairn has to prepare a barely edible dish using just a Pot Noodle, a box of Micro Chips and four cans of Super Lager.

2pm   **ANGELS WI MANKY COUPONS** *(film)*

4pm   **TAM THE TANK ENGINE**
Tam goes aff the rails and the Fat Controller gets chuffed tae bits.

4.15pm   **BOAB THE BUILDER**
Boab is investigated by the Inland Revenue.

4.30pm   **WINNIE THE SHITE**
Predictable cartoon capers from the bear with an unfortunate name.

5pm   **JOCK MacCRAVEN'S NEWSROOND**

5.05pm	**GOVAN HIGH** Children's drama set in a fictional Glasgow high school. This week Ryan chibs the heidmaister with a pincil while 13-year-old Chantelle reveals that she is expecting her fourth child.
5.30pm	**NEEBURS** Repeat showing of this eftirnin's episode.
6pm	**TEATIME NEWS AND WHAIR IT'S PISHIN DOON**
6.30pm	**TAP O' THE POPS 2** Grant Stott introduces hits from yesteryear. This week's show includes Van Morrison's 'Broon Yakked Lassie', 'Radge Wee Hing Cried Love' by Queen, 'When Doos Greet' by Prince and a live performance of the classic Dire Straits hit 'Hireys Fur Hee-Haw'.
7pm	**DOAKTIR WHAE** In this week's episode the Scottish time traveller takes the TARDIS back tae 1966 and breks Geoff Hurst's legs wae a sonic Glesca screwdriver.
7.30pm	**TORN FACED COCKNEY WANKERS** Eastenders wi' subtitles. In tonight's episode, Pauline gets her jotters fae the steamie while the rest of the cast

23

stoat aboot with faces the length of Leith Walk.

8pm **ONLY BAMS AND CUDDYS**
Feature length episode of the popular comedy. The cheeks of Deek-Boy's erse are knitting soaks when young Rab announces his new lemon curd works for the polis and the hoose is full tae the gunnells with chored DVD players. Meanwhile Uncle Hector runs into a spot of bother with the local neds who proceed to batter his melt in.

9pm **FITBA PLAYER'S BURDS**
Drama surrounding the players of fourth division Auchtermuchty Rovers and their off-pitch antics. This week Boaby is worried that the club is facing relegation while Moira is getting it baw deep from the Aberfeldy Academicals goalkeeper.

10pm **NEWS AND WHAIR IT'LL BE PISHIN DOON TH'MORN**

10.30pm **THE McOZBOURNES**
Reality TV show following the lives of failed Scottish rock star Hamish McOzbourne and his ugly family.

11.30pm **FITBA FAE HAMPDEN**
Highlights of this evening's match in

which Scotland take on the might of the Finland paperboy eleven. As always, the commentary is provided by Scottish football legend Kenny Dalglish and muckle chinned poofter Jimmy Hill.

12.30am   **MERRIT WI WEANS**
Re-make of the popular American sit-com 'Married With Children'. In this week's episode, Al sits in front of the telly scratchin his baws while Meg is still chokin oan her Nat King Cole.

1am   **POLIS**
Fly-on-the-wall documentary following the brave officers of Auchertool constabulary as they fight crime on a fortnightly basis.

1.30am   **THE BEECHGROVE BACK-GREEN**
The boys plans to dae up a gairdin in Niddrie, Edinburgh, are scuppered when local neds fuck off with the wheelbarra.

2am   **LATE CALL**
The Rev Alisdair Dreech reminds us that we are destined to burn in hell for all eternity.

2.15am   **CLOSEDOON**

6

CLAES

We all need clothes but when you consider the fashion capitals of the world it's highly unlikely that Scotland will figure in the top ten. You rarely hear the phrase New York, London, Paris, Methil. In fact, Scotland is in all probability the least fashionable country on earth with the possible exception of Wales. The climate and the deep-rooted cynicism possessed by the Scottish race as a whole has severely limited our flair for fashion and we prefer to adopt an attitude of practicality and financial prudence. After all, who in their right mind would pay £250 for a stylish designer bikini when the temperature on the beach at Aberdour rarely climbs beyond freezing.

In general, clothes are referred to as **Claes**, **Gear** or **Duds** and can be split into two basic categories. Anything worn on the torso is known as a **toap** (top) and anything below is known as **boatums** (bottoms). Here are the rest.

MEN'S UNDERWEAR
Trolleys, Scants, Keks, Drawers, Shreddies, Ys

WOMEN'S UNDERWEAR
Knickurs, Ankle-Warmers

VEST
Semmit

SOCKS
Soaks

BRACES
Galloshes

TROUSERS
Troosers, Breeks

SHIRT
Shurt

FOOTBALL TOP
Fitba toap

COAT
Jaikit

BOOTS
Bits

TRAINING SHOES
Gutties, Sannies, Plimpurs

PYJAMAS
Jammies

DRESSING GOWN
Goonie

APRON
Peenie

FLAT CAP
Bunnet

BASEBALL CAP
Basebaw cap

Most Scots will also own what is known as a **Guid Suit**. This will, at the very least, be a dress jacket and trousers, often of the same colour and cloth. It will, for the best part of the year, remain in the wardrobe only ever to be worn at weddings, funerals and the occasional court appearance.

7

SCRAN

Scotland has truly embraced international cuisine and now caters to all tastes – Chinese (sweet & sour chicken), Indian (curries), Middle Eastern (kebabs), American (happy meals) and Italian (white puddin supper).

The decline in demand for traditional Scottish fare can probably be linked to the fact that although, as a race, we Scots are capable of producing some of the finest food in the world, we are truly hopeless when it comes to giving dishes appealing names. Should you find yourself perusing the menu in a Scottish restaurant, you could be forgiven for thinking you were reading a copy of the well-known medical journal *The Lancet*.

Here are ten dishes which despite sounding like rare medical abnormalities are delicious and well worth experiencing.

CULLEN SKINK
Sounds like an inner-ear infection but it's a rich soup made with smoked haddock.

RUMBLEDETHUMPS
Sounds like an advanced case of glandular fever but it's a side dish of potatoes, cabbage and cheese.

CRANACHAN
Sounds like a skin disorder but it's a deliciously sweet dessert made with oatmeal, cream and Drambuie liqueur.

FINNAN HADDIE
Sounds like a sexually transmitted disease but it's the traditional name given to smoked haddock.

CLAPSHOT
Sounds like the cure for a bad case of Finnan Haddie but it's a side dish consisting of potatoes, turnip and chives.

STOVIES
Sounds like something guaranteed to get you out of school for a couple of weeks when you're young but it's a traditional Scottish dish made from potatoes, onions, beef dripping and is often served with sausages or corned beef.

COCK-A-LEEKIE
Sounds like a severe case of incontinence but it's a mouth-watering chicken and leek soup.

CLABBY DHU
Sounds like a painful swelling of the testicles but it's the name given to large mussels caught on the north east coast of Scotland.

HOWTOWDIE
Sounds like an erectile dysfunction but it's a roast chicken stuffed with oatmeal.

HAGGIS
Sounds like something that medical science managed to eradicate in the late 19th century but, in fact, it's best not to ask what the ingredients of the haggis consist of. Simply put your faith in God and enjoy its unique texture and taste.

If blood being allowed to flow freely through your arteries is the least of your worries, you might be tempted to sample some other uniquely Scottish delicacies.

THE FULL SCOTTISH BREAKFAST
Normally reserved for Sunday mornings, the full Scottish breakfast consists of:
Lorne sausage
a flat square sausage with oats rolled into the meat
black puddin
slices of congealed pig's blood
fruit puddin
raisins, currants and orange peel covered in suet
bacon
on no account should the fat be removed

These are all shallow fried in oil and served with as many fried eggs as you can eat. The whole dish is then smothered in either **rid sauce** (tomato ketchup) and/

31

or **broon sauce** (HP brown sauce) and washed down with a bottle of **Irn Bru** (a carbonated, fruit flavoured, soft drink known for its magical healing properties). It's always worth keeping a couple of Rennies or, if you have the means, a defibrillator on standby.

Another great Scottish tradition is the fish and chip shop or the **chippy** as it is more commonly known. The finest **chippys** are almost always run by Italians or those of Italian descent and offer good wholesome food – which they then coat in batter and deep fry – at a reasonable price. If you want to buy an item complete with chips you should ask for a **supper**. If you don't want chips, ask for a **single**. Here are a few of the items on offer at your local **chippy**:

PIE SUPPER
A traditional scotch pie containing meat of indeterminable origins which is deep fried and served with chips.

STEAK PIE SUPPER
Similar to the Scotch pie but with a filling which is slightly more recognisable. Again the entire pie is deep fried and served with chips.

SPECIAL FISH
Exactly the same kind of fish as its less special counterpart but coated with breadcrumbs as opposed to batter.

WHITE PUDDIN SUPPER
A sausage shaped pudding made with oatmeal and suet, deep fried and served with chips. It is also sometimes known as a mealy puddin.

FRITTER
A slice of potato which is coated in flour and batter then deep fried.

PIZZA SUPPER
A thin pre-prepared pizza with a simple cheese and tomato topping which is then deep fried and served with chips.

MARS BAR SUPPER
The popular chocolate bar is coated in batter and flash fried before being served with chips. There was a brief craze for these a few years ago and several chippys took it a step further by offering deep fried Creme Eggs, Bountys and Snicker Bars. They have become something of a rarity these days but as most **chippys** stock all the ingredients as a matter of course you could always ask the proprietor to make one specially for you if it is no longer on the menu.

Depending on the location of the chippy you will be asked if you would prefer salt & vinegar or salt & sauce on your food. Glaswegians and those on the West coast seem to prefer vinegar whereas in Edinburgh and Fife they prefer sauce which is similar to HP brown sauce but thinner in consistency and with a slightly sharper taste.

Here are a few helpful phrases to assist you, should you decide to eat out.

Ah could fair go fur some scran.
I feel a little peckish.

Ah'm pure Hank Marvin.
I am rather hungry.

Ah could eat a scabby hoarse a'tween two pishy mattresses.
I am absolutely ravenous.

There's hee-haw worth heckin in the hoose. Moan, lits treat wursels n' go oot.
There is very little choice in the pantry. Come on, let's treat ourselves by eating out this evening.

Huv ye goat a table fur two.
Do you have a table for two.

Geez wan near the windae n' well way fae the cludgy.
Can I have a table near the window but not too near the bathroom.

Any chance o' a swally afore ye dae any'hin else.
We would like to order some drinks straight away.

Geez a wee deek at the me-an-you.
Can I see a menu?

Haw Dafty, this soups baltic.
Excuse me waiter but my soup appears to be cold.

See the steak. Whit sauces dae ye dae wi it?
I have a question regarding the steak. Is it served with a choice of sauces?

Huv ye no goat rid or broon?
Don't you have any tomato ketchup or HP sauce?

Keep the swally comin.
We would like to order some more drinks.

Dae ye fancy a puddin?
Shall we order dessert?

That wiz rerr.
I thoroughly enjoyed that.

That wiz boggin.
The food really wasn't up to much.

Right, whits the damage?
Could we have the bill, please?

Away tae fuck! Sixty bar fur that? Away n' huv anither go it yer sums.
The bill seems to be awfully high. Would you mind checking it again?

Right ah'm gonnae kid oan ah'm no weel. In the stramash, you go n' dreep oot the bog windae, ah'll dae a runner n' then ah'll see ye back it the hoose.

I am going to cause a distraction by feigning illness. In the confusion you can make your escape by climbing out of the bathroom window. I will then abscond without paying the bill and will meet you back at home.

8

COURTIN

So you've got your eye on a charming young lady and you want to impress your friends with your impeccable taste. Here are a few phrases that will leave them in no doubt as to your intentions.

Git a swatch o' the lemon staunin oo'er thair nixt tae the puggy.
Have a look at the girl standing over there next to the fruit machine.

Jeezo, whit a stoater, eh?
Gosh she is an attractive young lady, isn't she?

Deek the paps oan ur, she looks like she's smugglin peanuts in ur bra.
Look at her shapely breasts, and her nipples are clearly visible.

Ye could hing a duffell coat wi a boatle o' Irn Bru in each poakit oan the end o' mine the noo.
I already have an erection.

Ah'd love tae tear the hole oaf that.
I certainly would consider myself fortunate to have sexual intercourse with her.

Ah love ridin burds.
I am 100% heterosexual, you understand.

First impressions are so important and you only get one chance to make them. Here are a few phrases which will have the ladies running out to buy dehumidifiers for their knicker drawer.

Awright doll, howzitgaun? Ma names (_____),
whits yours?
Hello, how do you do? Allow me to introduce myself.

Oan yer ain ur ye?
Are you alone this evening?

Yin wi yer pals, ur ye?
Are you here with friends?

Fancy a wee bevy?
Can I buy you a drink?

Fancy a wee jig?
Would you care to dance?

If you have got this far without having a drink thrown in your face (in certain areas of Glasgow this is closely followed by the glass it came from) you're pretty much on to a sure thing. But don't forget to keep that kettle boiling. Here are a few phrases to fill those long awkward silences.

Whit dae ye dae?
So what line of work are you in?

Aye good.
Really? That's interesting.

Whair ye fae?
Where do you live?

Nah, yev goat me scoobied thair. Mind you ah've nivir been further thin hauf an oor's staggerin distance fae ma ain hoose.
I'm not familiar with that area. I'm afraid I'm not terribly well travelled.

Whit did ye say yer name wiz again?
I'm awfully sorry but I appear to have forgotten your name.

Mibbes ah'll git ye up fur another jig a bit later oan.
Perhaps I could trouble you for another dance before the evening is over.

Git that doon ye n' ah'll git thum in again.
Can I buy you another drink?

Dae ye fancy gaun fur some scran? The chippy's jist doon the road.
Would you like to come for a meal? I know this charming little Italian place nearby.

Any chance o' chummin ye hame?
I would consider it an honour if you allowed me to escort you home.

Ah still stey at hame wi ma auld dear n' she'd go daft if ah broat a lassie back.
I still live at home with my mother and I'm afraid she is still a little old fashioned.

Should the young lady deny your request then you should consider the courtship a failure before storming off in search of someone smaller than yourself to start a fight with. It is still, however, possible to walk away with your dignity intact.

Well git it right up ye then ya hackit faced boot. Yer probably a dyke anywey.
Oh well, never mind. I didn't find you particularly attractive anyway and I suspect that you may have issues concerning your sexuality.

If the young lady permits you to escort her home you may respond in the following manner but try to do so with discretion.

Gaun yersel ya dancer!
How fortunate.

How auld ur ye by the wey?
Can I just confirm that you are over sixteen years of age?

Nice hoose yev goat here.
What a charming home you have.

Yer gittin it baw deep the night sweetheart.
I do hope you weren't expecting any foreplay as you are going to be seriously disappointed in that department.

Tell ye whit, you gie me a gam an ah'll huv a wee growl at the badger fur ye.
Here's an offer you can't refuse. If you perform oral sex upon me then I will grudgingly reciprocate the favour afterwards.

Naw ah huvnae goat a welly. Diz it matter?
No, I'm afraid I don't carry condoms on me. I just assumed that you weren't all that concerned with taking precautions.

Gonnae bell eh's a fast black hame?
Would you be so kind as to call me a taxi to take me home?

41

9

DRUNK

No night out in Scotland would be complete without a serious investment in alcohol. The most common names given to alcohol in Scotland are **Swally**, **Peive**, **Bevy** or quite simply **Drink**. There are, however, several more colourful expressions used to describe liquor. These include **CHEEKY WATTER, FALLING DOWN JUICE, OUZO DESTRUCTO, BAD BOY'S LEMONADE, FIREWATER, THE SINGIN GINGER, BELLYWASHER, THE SAUCE** and **THE ELECTRIC SOUP.**

Alcoholic beverages bought from an off licence for consumption at home or more commonly on a park bench are known as a **Cairry oot, Cargo or Judas** (Judas Escariot = Carry out).

It's a well-known fact that Eskimos have more than twenty different words for snow. This is perfectly understandable when you consider that they are surrounded by the stuff for approximately 365 days of the year and it goes a long way towards making conversations a bit more interesting when you have more than one word to describe what you see every

time you look out of the igloo window. So it comes as no surprise to learn that the Scots have managed to come up with over sixty slightly more original euphemisms to describe something as common as the sight of a wobbly man. This list is by no means exhaustive but here are a few of the more common expressions used to describe the act of being in an advanced state of intoxication.

AWAY WI THE GOALIE

AW OO'ER THE SHOAP

BANJANAS

BEELIN

BEVIED

BIRLIN

BLADDERED

BLEEZIN

BLITZED

BUCKLED

CABBAGED

CATTLED

DISABLED

FAW'IN ABOOT

FLEEIN

FU

GUTTERED

GONE

HAMMERED

HOWLIN

HUD A SKINNFY

ILED UP

IN NAE FIT STATE

JAKED

JOOKED

LEATHERED

MIRACULOUS

MORTAL

MUNTED

NUGGETS

OAF THE MAP

OAN THE SAUCE

OOTAY IT

OOT YER FACE

OOT YER TREE

PARALYTIC

PEEVED

PICKLED

PIE EYED

PISHED

PISHED AS A FART

PLASTERED

RAT-ARSED

REEKIN
REELIN
RUBBERED
SLIGHTLY INEBRIATED
SMEEKIT
SOZZLED
SPARKOED
SLAUGHTERED
SMASHED
STEAMIN
STEAMBOATS
STEWED
STOATIN
SUITABLY REFRESHED
TANKED UP
THREE SHEETS TAE THE WIND
UNABLE TO BITE ONE'S AIN FING-UR
WASTED
WELL GONE
WELL ILED
WELLIED
WRECKED
ZOMBIFIED

It's enough to make you thirsty . . .

10

GLASWEGIAN RHAPSODY

Once you're well iled, here's a good way to make a real impression on your night out. This parody of the classic Queen song 'Bohemian Rhapsody' has been doing the rounds on the internet for many years. It seems almost impossible to track down the original author so instead it seems only fair to credit the late great Freddie Mercury for its inspiration and the good people of Glasgow for the slang.

Glaswegian Rhapsody

Is this the real life? Is this the methadone?
Stuck in the Gorbals wi two bob fur the telephone
Open yer wine an talk wi a whine like me
Ah'm jist a Weegie, gie us yer Sunny D
Cos ah'll chib yer pal, rip yer da
Slash yer dug, ride yer ma
Anywey the Clyde flows, disnae really matter,
Tae me
Tae me

Haw Maw! Jist chibbed some bam
Buckie boatle roond the hied
Noo the silly basturt's deid
Haw Maw! Ah'm jist oot oan parole
An noo ah'm headin back tae the Bar-L
Haw Maw! Oo-oo-oo-ooooh
Didnae mean tae dae um in
If ah'm no full o' skag this time the morra
Cairry oot, Cairry oot
Then we'll go oot oan the batter

Too late, the bailiff's here
Sendin shivers doon ma spine
Gubbed ten jellies jist in time
Cheerio ma muckers, ah've goat tae go
Goat tae go an rip some wide cunt fae the scheme
Haw Maw! Oo-oo-oo-ooooh
Ah'm a jakey bam
Ah sometimes think ah've nivir been washed at aw

(nasal cattarh solo)

Ah see a little silhouetto of a bam
Adidas, Adidas, can ye go get us a cargo
Thunderbird, White Lightning
Very very frightening, tae me
Twenty Mayfair, Twenty Mayfair
Twenty Mayfair, Twenty Mayfair
Twenty Mayfair an some skins
Magnifico oh oh oh oh oh
Ah'm jist a fat boy fae a fat family
He's just a fat boy fae a fat family

48

Spare us ten bob fur a hot cup o' tea
Git tae fuck ya manky slob, go an get a job
Fur fuck's sake, No! Ah'll no git a joab
Get a job
Fur fuck's sake, No! Ah'll no git a joab
Get a job
Ah'll no git a joab
Get a job
Ah'll nivir git a joab. No. No. No. No. No.
Gonorrhoea, Gonorrhoea, Gonorrhoea and a dose
Then doon the pub whair the barman's goat a pint
fur me, fur me, fur meeeeeeeee

So ye think ye can slash me an pish in ma eye
So ye think ye can chib me an leave me tae die
Haw baw-bag! Can't dae that tae me baw-bag
Jist wait till ah'm oot, wait till ah'm right ootay here
Hee-haw really matters, any cunt can see
Hee-haw really matters
Hee-haw really matters tae me

Anywey the Clyde flows

Pure quality.

11

PAGGERS

Contrary to popular belief, Scotland is no more prone to acts of mindless violence than any other part of the United Kingdom. The city streets of Edinburgh, Glasgow, Dundee and Aberdeen are no different to the city streets of London, Liverpool, Birmingham and Cardiff at 2 o'clock on a Sunday morning. That is to say, that they are populated by hordes of young men whose alcohol to testosterone ratio is at its critical peak.

Fighting in the street has for a long time been commonplace in Scotland and the current trend for binge drinking coupled with an ever growing knife culture shows no signs of improving in the near future.

Looking on the bright side, however, despite an increase in gun crimes, the chances of being gunned down in a drive-by shooting on the streets of Scotland are still pretty slim.

Here are ten handy tips which could save you from spending the evening in a casualty department having shards of broken glass removed from your face.

1. Avoid pubs with pool tables. This game seems to encourage violence and comes complete with its own vast array of offensive weapons.

2. Never argue with bouncers. If a bouncer has already refused you entry to an establishment, he or she is unlikely to be persuaded to change their mind by casting aspersions on their parentage, sexual orientation or personal hygiene. Be honest, when *was* the last time you heard a bouncer say, 'You know, now I come to think of it, I am a smelly, poofy basturt. In you go then.'

3. Be aware of your surroundings and try not to spill anyone's drink. Nine out of ten fights in pubs begin with an overturned beverage of some description.

4. Don't speak to anyone while standing at the urinal in the toilet. Even an acknowledging nod of the head can be seen as a flagrant display of homosexuality.

5. Don't make eye contact with anyone in a chip shop queue after 11.30pm. This is where homicidal maniacs gather to feed.

6. Avoid discussing the English national football squad. Scottish history books have no record of the year 1966.

7. Avoid discussing football whatsoever, especially in Glasgow where religious bigotry is rife.

8. Avoid discussing religion. See No 7.

9. Avoid discussing politics. Always a sticky subject but more so if you have the misfortune to be a supporter of the Conservative Party. Margaret Thatcher is not held in high esteem and in the popularity stakes she comes somewhere in between Adolph Hitler and Jimmy Hill.

10. Invest in a good pair of running shoes. If trouble does flare up, the best advice is to run in the opposite direction as quickly as possible.

Defining a fight in Scottish slang depends on the scale, the ferocity of the fight itself and the relationship of those involved. First of all, there is verbal abuse.

SLAGGIN
The verbal ridicule of another is generally referred to as **slaggin thum oaf** or **gein thum pelters**. This can range from a **mild slaggin** in which the recipient is content to go along with the joke despite causing mild embarrassment, to **rippin the pish ootay thum** which is a substantially more aggressive form of ridicule.

Ye missed yersel last night in Clancy's. Norrie came back fae the bogs wi a wet penny in eh's poakit. Rab deeks um n' starts slaggin oaf. Norrie takes a beamer bit eh disnae seem aw'at baured. Rab keeps gaun n' Norrie starts tae bite noo. Rab really starts rippin

the pish ootay Norrie till eh fucks oaf in a huff. Ah dinnae mind Rab bit eh kin be a shan basturt when eh wants tae.

You really will kick yourself for not being present last night at Clancy's. Norman had returned from the bathroom with a small yet distinct urine stain upon the front of his trousers. Robert noticed this and began to make fun of Norman who despite the mild shame, took no offence. Robert continued to ridicule Norman who soon began to tire of the seemingly endless jibes at his expense and asked Robert to refrain from making any more. The snide remarks continued until Norman left in a sulk. I do admit to being fond of Robert but he does have a cruel sense of humour at times.

BOLLICKIN

The **bollockin** or, as it is sometimes referred to, a **sherakin** is a one-sided verbal attack in which the recipient has no option but to take it. For instance, a boss may be required to give an employee a severe dressing down for his general incompetence.

The high heid yin hud eh's in eh's oaffice this efternin fur a right bollickin. Tore me up fur erse paper tae. Ken whit eh says tae eh's? Eh says a couldnae keep a cat gaun in mulk. Ah tell ye, see if ah didnae need the hireys ah'd huv telt um tae ram eh's joab right up eh's Cameron Toll.

The manager called me into his office this afternoon and proceeded to inform me that my current attitude towards work was unacceptable. He then went on to question my ability to perform the simplest of tasks.

Were I not quite so reliant on my salary, I would have offered him my immediate resignation.

RAMMY
This refers to a heated exchange of two vastly opposed points of view and will more often than not contain a certain amount of profane language. These volatile discussions are also known as **barneys**, **ding-dongs** or **a stramash.**

A SET TO
If either party fails to diffuse the **rammy**, there is always the danger it could lead to **a set to** which is as far as an argument can be taken without resorting to actual physical violence. During **a set to** the participants will inflate their chests, clench their fists and try to outstare each other.

Tam n' Alec hud a bit o' a set to it dinner time. They'd been nigglin each other aw day when Tam went aff eh's nut. Ah thoat Alec wiz gonnae blooter um.
Thomas and Alexander almost came to blows at lunchtime. They had been getting under one another's skin all day when Thomas suddenly lost his temper. I thought for a moment that Alexander was about to strike him.

Actual physical violence can be described in a number of ways. A fair fight involving no more than two people and without the use of weapons is known as a **square go**. Sadly these have all but become a thing of the past and invariably the call for **handers** (assistance) will go out, which is an invitation for a free-for-all. Or a knife will be produced and some poor bugger ends up on a mortician's slab.

A fight which involves nothing more than the occasional pushing and shoving might be described as **a couple o' eejits dancin aboot the street like a perr o' fairies**, or **handbags at ten paces**.

A full on, all out physical assault is described as **a pagger, a swedge, a battle, a pummellin, a hidin', a healthy kickin** or **a right good doin'**.

Assuming this isn't a random assault in which you are attacked without warning, most **paggers** begin with a brief period in which the two combatants will pace around in a circle issuing elaborate threats towards one another. It is unclear weather this brief interlude is designed to give the opponents time to size each other up or harks back to a more chivalric time when it was considered the height of bad manners to strike an opponent before allowing him the opportunity to plan a counter attack. It's worth noting that at this point it is still possible to defuse the entire situation by running away. This may be taken as a slur on your masculinity and appear humiliating but as any doctor worth his salt will tell you, 'A bruised ego heals a damn sight quicker than a punctured lung.'

Some common threats to watch out for are:

Your tea's oot ya muppet.
It is my intention to physically assault you.

Dae ye hink ah'm feared o' you? Come ahead ya prick.
Challenge accepted.

Ah'm gonnae gie ye a smack in the pus.
I intend to deliver an open handed blow to your face that is intended to cause you more in the way of humiliation than actual physical pain.

Ah'm gonnae tan yer jaw.
I intend to deliver a blow to the side of your face that will leave a mark not too dissimilar to a mild case of sunburn.

Ah'm gonnae gie ye a burst mooth.
I intend to punch you in the face leaving you with superficial injuries to the mouth.

Ah'm gonnae gie ye a dull yin.
I intend to punch you in the face, leaving you dazed and disorientated for a brief period of time.

Ah'm gonnae deck ye.
I intend to punch you in the face in the hope that you will fall over and remain in a prone position.

Ah'm gonnae fit yer erse.
I intend to give you a kick up the backside.

Ah'm gonnae stick ma tae up yer crevice.
I intend to kick you up the backside with a great deal of force.

Ah'm gonnae stick ma boot that far up yer erse folk'll start hinkin Doc Martin makes hats.
I intend to kick you up the backside with sufficient force to lead observers of your predicament to believe that my boot is some new brand of headwear.

Ah'm gonnae batter yer melt in.
I intend to deliver several blows to your head and body.

Ah'm gonnae boot fuck ootay ye.
I intend to kick you about the head and body with enough severity as to cause internal bleeding.

Ah'm gonnae ram the nut oan ye.
I intend to strike you across the bridge of your nose with the full force of my forehead.

Ah'm gonnae stove yer heid in.
I intend to fracture your skull either with my fist or the use of a blunt instrument of some description.

Ah'm gonnae boot yer baws oot the back o' yer heid.
I intend to kick you in the testicles with sufficient force to send them on an upwards trajectory before exiting through a hole in the back of your head.

Ah'm gonnae gie ye the severe malky.
I intend to use a knife or similar sharpened implement to create a wound requiring immediate medical attention to your face.

Ah'm gonnae chib ye.
I intend to use a knife or similar sharpened implement to stab you.

Ah'm gonnae dae ye in.
I intend to murder you.

Assuming you are a witness rather than a combatant in the ensuing melée, you may want to offer encouragement or perhaps tactical advice to either opponent. These phrases are intended for that very purpose.

Whae dae ye fancy?
Who do think will emerge victorious?

Deek that yin. Eh's built like a brick shithoose.
Look at that chap in particular. He certainly is a large fellow.

Aye bit the ithir yin looks a bit o' a bam tae me. It widnae surprsise me if he hud a chib in eh's back poakit.
Yes I agree, but his opponent has the look of a homicidal maniac. I wouldn't be in the least bit surprised if he was concealing some kind of knife on his person.

Aw! Here we go.
I see they have started fighting.

C'moan big yin. Git tore intae um.
Hooray for the larger of the two. Now hit him with all your might.

Git up wee man! Go fur eh's baws.
Get back on your feet smaller of the two. Try to take advantage by kicking him repeatedly in the testicles.

Finish the wee fanny oaf. Gie um wan wi the bunnet n' two wi the berr heid.
Teach this little upstart a lesson by head-butting him.

Perhaps you are abhorred by violence and wish to put an end to this common street brawl. If so, you may wish to use one of the following expressions:

Aw gie it up yous two, fur fuck's sake.
Come on you two, let's put an end to this nonsense.

Leave um alane, wull ye?
Please refrain from hitting him again.

Ye'll both end up gittin huckled.
Should the police happen upon this skirmish it is likely that you will both be taken into custody.

The carrying of offensive weapons is becoming more prevalent and, as is often the case in **paggers**, there is always a real danger that at some point a knife may be produced.

Aw fuck! The wee felly's goat a chib. Ah telt ye eh wiz a bammer.
Goodness me. The smaller chap is now brandishing a knife. Did I not say that he looked the dangerous sort?

Lits shoot the craw afore the polis git here.
I think it would be for the best if we moved along before the local constabulary are alerted to the situation.

Should the police arrive at the scene of an assault that you were witness to, you may be required to give a brief statement.

Thirs nae point asking me anyhin, ah saw hee-haw.
I cannot help you as I didn't actually see the attack take place.

Ah saw the two guys swedging.
I witnessed the assault.

It sterted oaf is a square go bit the big felly wiz giein the wee guy a right hiding. Then the wee guy pulls a chib oot eh's back poakit n' gave the big felly the severe malky.
It began as a fair fight between both men. The larger of the two had a distinct advantage and was delivering a series of painful looking blows to the smaller man's body. It was at this point that the smaller chap produced a knife and assaulted the larger chap by slashing him across the face.

61

The big felly went doon like a sack o' tatties an the wee guy bolted doon that road.
The large chap collapsed to the ground and his attacker fled in that general direction at great speed.

Whit dae ye need ma name fur?
I have told you all I can tell you. I can see no earthly reason why you should need to take down my particulars.

Ah'm no comin the cunt. Ah jist dinnae want tae gie ye ma name.
I can assure you that it is not my intention to be uncooperative. It's just that should this be taken any further, I would rather not become involved.

Whit the fuck ur ye liftin me fur?
Why am I being apprehended?

So, if you end up in police custody now, you only have yourself to blame.

12

BEGGARS

Twenty years ago it was so much easier to spot a beggar in Scotland as they all wore long shabby grey overcoats. They also had noses that resembled huge over-ripe strawberries and had long bushy beards that contained crumbs and small things with lots of legs. They would perform clumsy **jigs** (dances) and play barely recognisable tunes on their **moothies** (harmonicas) before extending their **bunnet** (flat cap) to accept a few coins from grateful passers-by. Once they had accumulated the required amount of cash for a bottle of cheap cooking sherry, they would get smashed out of their skulls and argue with invisible people before passing out in some urine soaked shop doorway.

Mass unemployment and the introduction of the one pound coin in the 1980s transformed begging into a highly competitive industry. The hobos of yesteryear were soon replaced by a younger, more dynamic beggar. According to certain tabloid newspapers, these derelict yuppies were coining in hundreds of pounds a day and turning up for work in sports cars.

These days you can find the aggressive beggar in any major Scottish city centre, usually around bus and railway stations where they regale passers-by with grossly exaggerated tales of woe in exchange for loose change. Here's what you should expect:

Skuze me, pal.
Excuse me my friend.

This is the traditional opening gambit used by the beggar in an attempt to part you from your hard earned cash. It's your last chance to walk away and you should be aware that any further involvement will lead to one of two conclusions. At best, it will cost you upwards of 50p or, in the worst case scenario, you will receive an earful of obscenities casting doubt on your parentage and sexual orientation.

Yenny sperr change oan ye pal?
Could you spare me any loose change you may have about your person?

Ye couldnae sperr us a few shillins fur a cuppy tea, coodgie?
Would you like to donate an unspecified amount of cash towards the price of a hot drink?

Ah couldnae tap a couple o' quid oaf ye coodah? Ah've loast ma bus ferr n' ah need tae git hame tae git the weans tea oan.
Would you be so kind as to spare me £2. I have mislaid the money I had originally set aside to pay

for my bus fare home and I fear that my children will go hungry if I am unable to return in time to prepare their main evening meal.

Ah've hud hee-haw tae scran fur days. Gonnae geez a dig oot?
A great deal of time has passed since my last square meal and I was wondering if you would be so kind as to help me in a financial sense.

Ma auld dear's up the hoaspitul n'ah wiz wantin tae git ur some flooers.
My dear silver-haired mother is in hospital and I fear her poor heart would break if I were to visit her without a floral gift of some description. Unfortunately, due to circumstances beyond my control I am without sufficient funds to purchase said flowers and failure on

PLEASE HELP

EX-LEMON CURD AND 4 WEANS TAE FEED, £250 FINE FUR CHORIN OOTAY WOOLIES TAE PEY, THE REPAYMENTS OAN 42 INCH FLAT SCREEN TELLY TAE KEEP UP, SAVING UP FUR SKY SPORTS.

I ACCEPT CASH, CHEQUES AND ALL MAJOR CREDIT CARDS.

THANK YOU

your part to assist me financially could result in her imminent demise and I am sure you wouldn't wish the death of my mother on your conscience. (Beggars will often play on the sympathies of others to obtain cash.)

Kinna cadge a fag oaf ye?
Could I scrounge a cigarette from you?

Kinna buy a fag oaf ye?
Could I scrounge a cigarette from you?
(Despite the offer to pay for said cigarette, the beggar has no intention of actually parting with any money and a demand of recompense would be an act of futility in itself.)

If the beggar has managed to persuade you into giving him any money, your main objective is to now employ a delaying tactic in which you can fumble around for the smallest amount of change in your pockets. Remember that pound coins have milled edges and 50p pieces have odd-shaped sides so try and feel for smooth round coins. There are a few phrases you can use to stall for time.

Aye, nae baur.
Yes, that will be no problem.

A'ts aw ah've goat.
I'm afraid it's not much but it really is all I can spare.

Mind n' no blaw that oan swally/skag.
Take this small amount of cash but please don't squander it on alcohol/heroin.

If the beggar has failed to persuade you into handing over any money there are several responses you can give. The easiest is to simply ignore them or display the universal sign for 'I have no spare change' by adopting a sympathetic expression, patting your trouser pockets and extending your empty palms. Alternatively you could try any of the following:

No the'day.
Not today. (This helps to appease any guilt you may be feeling by offering the beggar a modicum of false hope that you may giving him something tomorrow or at some later date.)

Ah'm borassic masel.
I'm afraid that I am unable to offer assistance as I too am without any legal tender.

Wayne work!
I have no money to give you and I recommend that you find yourself gainful employment in order to support yourself.

Git you away tae buggery ya poachin basturt!
I certainly have no intention of giving you any money, you workshy layabout. I suggest you remove yourself and take up residence elsewhere.

Away you an fling shite at yersel!
Taken literally this is an instruction to go away and throw excrement at yourself but translates as 'Absolutely not'.

Not being the brightest of girls, Donna took the news of acute angina as a compliment and asked if she could have a wee keek at the doctor's clackerbag.

13

HEALTH

Many of the health-related issues you'll come across will be directly related to the effects of strong drink, fighting and sex. Here are a few phrases you may find helpful if you are concerned about health issues, starting with how to enquire into how someone is feeling.

Huv ye hud a faw?
Did you fall over?

Yer lookin gey peely-wally. Ur you feelin awright?
You look rather pale. How do you feel?

Ur ye gonnae boak up?
Do you feel as though you are going to be sick?

Ah'm gonnae git a basin.
You look as though you are going to be sick. I think I should go and fetch a receptacle of some kind.

Ah swear tae fuck. If you spew up aw oo'er ma good cairpit, ah'll go fuckin radge.
If you are going to be sick, please make sure you use the receptacle I have offered you. I would be most upset should you get any vomit on my carpet.

Aye, yuv split yer heid open.
As I expected, you have suffered a small cut to the head.

Minny fing-urs um ah huddin up?
How many fingers am I holding up?

Nineteen? Ur ye aff yer nut?
Hmmm. I think you have sustained a slight concussion.

Ah dinnae like the look o' ye. Ah'm gonnae git the doaktir in tae huv a wee deek it ye.
I am concerned by your current deterioration in health. I think I ought to seek medical attention on your behalf.

Gonnae sit doon afore ye faw doon.
I think it might be best if you sat down, just in case you start to feel a little faint.

The following phrases are intended to alert others to your general state of health and at this point in time there is probably no need to visit a doctor.

Ah feel a wee bit wabbit.
I feel slightly unwell.

70

Ah'm no weel.
I feel unwell.

Ah feel as seek as a dug.
I feel extremely unwell.

Ah hink ah'm gittin a cauld.
I think I may be catching a cold.

Ah've goat a snottery beak.
I have a runny nose.

Ma heid's pure nippin.
I have a headache.

Ah hink ah'm gonnae keel oo'er.
I feel faint.

Ah've been spewin ma ring up.
I have been violently sick.

Ah hink ah've goat a dose o' the Tex Ritters comin oan.
I fear a sudden attack of diahorrea may be imminent.

Aw naw! Ah've jist kakked ma splodgers.
Oh dear. I have just fouled myself.

Ma Duke O' Argyll's ur gein me gyp n' ma holes rid raw.
My haemorrhoids are causing me a great deal of discomfort and my anus is inflamed.

71

Should you feel the need to visit the doctor's surgery or the accident and emergency department, the following phrases may be helpful.

Ah took a heider doon the sterrs n' tanned ma leg. Ah've been hirplin aboot ivir since n' ah hink a might need a stookie.
I took a tumble down the stairs and hurt my leg. I have been limping ever since and I think it may require a plaster cast.

Ma nixt door neeburs dug sank it's wallies intae ma erse. Um a gonnae need a jag?
My next door neighbour's dog bit me on the bottom. Will this require an injection?

Ah wiz huvin a bit o' a barney wi the burd. Ah called her a poke-nosed howk n' she wrapped a nine iron roond ma napper.
I had a difference of opinion with my wife. I said something to upset her and she struck me across the head with a golf club.

Ah goat set aboot oan bi a team o' neds n' wan o' the wee fannies chibbed eh's in the shooder.
I was attacked by a gang of juvenile delinquents and one those cowardly thugs has stabbed me in the shoulder.

Zat gonnae leave a mars bar?
Will this leave me permanently scarred?

Depending on the nature of your complaint, seeking medical assistance can often lead to a certain amount of embarrassment. Honesty is normally the best policy and no matter how bad the situation, the medical staff will always treat your condition in confidence and with the utmost discretion. That is, until you have left the premises, when you will be mercilessly ridiculed by the doctors, nurses and various other hospital orderlies.

A couple o' weeks ago, ah' noticed a wee plook oan the end o' ma walloper. It's noo the size o' a tumshie n' startin tae honk like buggery. Is it gonnae drap aff?
Two weeks ago, I noticed a small pimple on the tip of my penis. It has since grown to the size of a turnip and is giving off a rather pungent aroma. Is this a cause for concern?

Ah wiz wae a shelter-belter oan Friday night n' ivir since, ah've been clawin ma baws like fuck. Ah' hink ah' might huv a dose.
I had sex with a girl of low self esteem in a bus shelter on Friday evening and ever since, I have been experiencing prolonged itching of the testicles. I think I may have contracted a sexually transmitted disease.

Yer no gonnae stick that brolly jag up ma japs yak, ur ye?
I do hope the stories concerning the treatment of venereal diseases have been grossly exaggerated.

Honest tae fuck. Ah wiz oan the bog when the phone goes. Ah pulls ma troosers back up but ah furgoat tae dae up ma ballop. Ah bolt doonstairs tae git the phone when troosers n' keks faw doon n' ah lands right oan toap o' a boatle o' ginger thit some muppet's left in the middle o' the flair. Lucky fur me, it didnae brek bit the hing is, it went right up ma jeer. Ah tried tae git it oot masel bit a hink ah made it worse. Any chance ye could git it oot fur eh's eh?

I swear that the story I am about to tell is true. I was sitting on the toilet when I heard the telephone ring. I got up, adjusted my clothing but must have omitted to fasten my flies in my rush to answer the telephone. My trousers and underpants fell down and I tripped. I landed on top of a bottle of carbonated soft drink which some thoughtless person had left lying on the floor in the middle of the room. Thankfully the bottle remained intact saving me from serious lacerations. What was unfortunate is that the bottle entered my rectum. I did my best to retrieve the bottle but I think I may have exacerbated the situation. Could you please remove it as it is causing a great deal of discomfort.

Alternatively you could save a lot of time and unnecessary embarrassment with this simpler phrase.

Right doc, I've awready goat a beamer bit here's the Hampden. I've stuck a boatel o' ginger up ma hole n' noo ah cannae get it oot again. Gonnae dae eh's a turn?

74

Well doctor, this is already causing me a great deal of embarrassment. l feel I have to be honest with you so I won't waste your time with silly excuses. I have, for my own reasons, inserted a bottle of carbonated soft drink into my rectum and now find myself in a rather embarrassing situation in that, no matter how hard I have tried, I am unable to retrieve it. Would you be so kind as to help me with the minimum amount of fuss?

It would be highly unlikely that the doctor who attends you speaks in slang, but as we approach a more classless society, it might help to be prepared. Here are a few phrases a doctor might use to determine the treatment you require.

S'up wi you then?
What appears to be the problem.

Oh, ya bugger! That looks sair.
That does look like a painful wound.

Stoap greetin ya big jessie.
Take deep breaths and try to calm down.

Dinnae worry. Ye'll be ripped oot yer tits in a minute.
I'm going to give you something for the pain.

Yawright noo?
Does that feel better?

Hud ye been oan the swally when ye took a heider.
Had you been drinking when you fell over.

Whit dae ye pit away a week?
On average, what would you say your weekly intake of alcohol was?

Fuck me! Ya jakey basturt!
Goodness me, that is a lot. I assume you have alcohol related disorders.

You keep gaun the wey yer gaun n' ye'll huv copped yer whack afore the endy the year.
I feel I ought to warn you that if you do not seek professional help to confront your alcoholism you could in all honesty be dead by Christmas.

Again, honesty is the best policy where doctors are concerned and should you find yourself in a situation in which you have no one but yourself to blame, it's beneficial to all concerned to come clean.

Look ye kin spraff that pish aw ye like, bit lit's no kid wursells oan. Noo the longer you keep gein me this pish, the longer it's gonnae take fur me tae fun whitivir it is ye stuck up yer ain jeer n' git it oot again.
I'm not particularly interested in how it got there, but I feel it would be remiss of me not to remind you that until we have identified the foreign object lodged in your rectum, the more prolonged your discomfort will be.

14

FITBA

The main thing to remember about football is that there are three distinctly different types of football fans that inhabit Scotland. First of all there is the fan who turns up on the terraces every Saturday come rain or shine and enjoys the spectacle of the game itself with nothing more than a mutton pie and a steaming hot cup of Bovril to make the afternoon complete. These people are generally dull, unimaginative and warrant no further mention.

Then there's the world famous 'Tartan Army'. Easily identified by their uniform, (kilt, football shirt and **see you jimmy** hat) over-developed sense of optimism and their inability to remain vertical for prolonged periods of time, these crack troops can be deployed to any part of the globe' at a moment's notice to witness the national squad suffer yet another humiliating defeat while at the same time ensuring that the owners of local bars and taverns can afford to buy speedboats, private jets and send their children to outrageously expensive schools. Unlike their English counterparts, the Tartan Army's friendly reputation precedes them and they are almost always ensured the warmest of welcomes abroad.

This brings us to the last, and thankfully least numerous, type of fan – the ninety minute bigot, who falls into one of two categories. The Catholic bigot will follow Celtic Football Club, adorn himself in the colours of the Irish Republican flag and sing Irish rebel songs glorifying the IRA, which are far from flattering to the ears of Rangers supporters.

The Protestant bigot will follow Glasgow Rangers, adorn himself in the colours of the Union Jack and sing loyalist songs which praise King Billy. This in turn seems to upset the Celtic supporters.

A football match involving both teams is known as an **Auld Firm Gemme** and is nothing more than an excuse for the opposing supporters to vent spleen for an hour and a half. The Celtic fans particularly enjoy casting aspersions on the sexual antics of the Queen of England whereas the Rangers fans prefer to cast doubts on the sexual orientation of the Bishop of Rome.

There is a theory that the fans who partake in sectarian bigotry do so to hide their general ignorance of the game itself. With an IQ only slightly higher than the average cheese sandwich they can hardly be expected to grasp a highly complex scenario involving 22 men trying to kick a ball into one of two previously designated ends of a field. Ashamed of their own limited intelligence and not wishing to be mistaken for homosexuals, they diligently turn up on match days to scream banal obscenities at each other for a full ninety minutes.

If someone enquires as to whether you are a **Billy** or a **Dan**, they are asking if you are a protestant (**Billy**) or a Catholic (**Dan**).

Both sets of fans have a variety of names for each other, some of which they find more offensive than others, although this depends solely on who is addressing them.

CELTIC FANS	RANGERS FANS
Dan	Billy
Tim	Billy-Boy
Jungle Jim	Proddy
Pape	Hun
Green grape	Blue-Nose
Fenian basturt	Orange basturt
Bhoy	Teddy bear
Left fitter	Currant Bun
	(rhyming slang for hun)
Taigs	DOBs (which stands for
	dirty orange basturt)

These phrases are normally sandwiched between the word **Filthy** and **Basturt** and they can and frequently do refer to each other as **Soap-Dodgers, Mankies** and **Scum bags**.

If you don't fit into any of the categories above, make sure you keep your running shoes handy just in case.

15

TAXIS

Public transport in Scotland is undoubtedly excellent but after a night out who wants to stand at the bus stop for an hour waiting for a night bus which may or may not turn up? In the wee small hours there's only really one option and taxis in Scotland are generally referred to as a **fast black** or a **Joe Baxi**.

Dae ye fancy grabbin a fast black up the toon?
Would you like to take a taxi into the city centre?

Nah. Ah'm pratted. It's shanks's pony fur me.
No. I can't afford to take a taxi and will have to walk instead.

Ah'm too cattled tae hoof it aw the wey hame. Lits grab a Joe.
I am far too drunk to attempt walking home. Let's take a taxi.

Huz that yin goat it's light oan?
Does that one appear to be for hire?

At the taxi rank:

Anybiddy wantae go haufers oan a taxi tae (insert destination here)
Would anyone like to split the fare to (insert destination here)

Haw! thurz a queue here ya choob.
Excuse me but there are other people besides yourself waiting for a taxi.

Hailing a taxi:

HO!
Taxi!

Generic insults directed towards taxi drivers who ignore your attempts to hail them.

Ur ye fuckin blint?
Are you blind?

Wayne git a joab ye like ya prick.
If driving a taxi causes you such displeasure, why not find alternative employment?

Gittit right up ye ya fanny!
Can't you see that I am trying to hire your cab?

Wair you gaun ya baw-bag?
Why, in the name of all that is holy, won't you stop?

Taxi drivers are often reluctant to pick up males who appear to be drunk. The last thing a hard working cabbie needs is to waste his valuable time mopping up the contents of someone's stomach. The chances of hailing a cab are greatly increased if you are not staggering around in the middle of the road waving your arms in the air and screaming like a banshee. For some inexplicable reason taxi drivers are not quite so fussy about picking up females who are in an advanced state of intoxication.

If you do find yourself a little the worse for wear, it's best to try and appear as sober as humanly possible until you are seated in the cab with the door closed firmly behind you. Then, you have a range of possible options:

Takeys tae (insert destination here).
Take me to (insert destination here).

Takeys tae the nearest rub shoap.
Take me to the nearest brothel masquerading as a massage parlour.

Kinna stoap oaf fur fags/a chippy?
Would you mind making a brief stop on the way home so that I may purchase cigarettes/something to eat?

Geez a shout when the meter gits tae six bar.
Could you alert me to when the meter reaches six pounds. (If you try to make yourself sound as pathetic as possible when saying this, you may be lucky enough to encounter a taxi driver sympathetic to your plight who will drive you all the way home for only six pounds.)

Zit awright if a scran ma kebab?
Do you mind if I eat my kebab in the back of your cab?

Zit awright if ah spark up?
Do you mind if I smoke?

Whit if ah pit the windae doon?
Would it be permissible to smoke if I wind the window down?

Whit if ah lean ma napper oot the windae?
Would it be permissible to smoke if I kept the window open and leant my head out of the taxi altogether?

Awright, keep the heid, ah'm pittin it oot.
Very well, there is no need to adopt such a hostile attitude. I will extinguish the cigarette.

As with barbers, it is customary to engage taxi drivers in banal conversation on the way to your destination. Both the following phrases are suitable for kick starting some kind of rapport:

Huv ye been busy th'night?
Has business been good this evening?

Whit time ye oan tae?
At what time does your current shift terminate?

You may encounter certain problems when hiring a taxi after a night out, especially if you are feeling unwell or lack ready funds. The following phrases are designed to deal with the more common situations:

Huv we no been doon this road twice afore awready, ya fuckin footpad?
Haven't we already taken this route. I believe you are trying to extort a higher fare from me.

Litties oot. Ah hink ah'm gonnae boak.
Can you stop and let me out as I think I am about to be sick.

Turn the meter oaf an ah'll gie ye a gam whin we git tae whair wur gaun.
If you take me all the way home without charge, I will perform fellatio upon you when we reach our destination. (This normally only works with female passengers, but you never know until you try.)

Jist littlies oot here.
Can you drop me off here.

Jist littlies oot oan the corner.
Can you drop me off at the corner.

Jist littlies out at the fit o' that close.
Can you drop me off at the entrance to that narrow passage.

Ah'll jist need tae nip up the sterrs fur yer hireys.
Perhaps I should have made this clear when I first hired your cab, but at this current moment in time I am without sufficient funds to pay the fare. If you would be so kind as to unlock the door, I shall go upstairs and return with the required amount of money including a substantial tip for yourself.

Haw, yer bumped!
That will teach you not to be so gullible in future, I had no intention of paying you and now I am going to make good my escape, safe in the knowledge that you will never catch me. (It's best to make sure that you are well out of the taxi and a considerable distance away before making this statement.)

16

BODY PARTS

If you don't know your body parts by now, how will you ken yer erky fae yer elby? Here are several slang words to choose from when describing the various parts of the **boady**. Certain areas of the human anatomy have more than their fair share of alternative names though it seems that inspiration dries up once we have travelled south of the backside.

HEAD
Heid, Napper, Scone, Bonce, Skull, Nut, Pan-Loaf.

FACE
Coupon, Fizog, Fizzer, Melt.

EYES
Yaks, Keekers.

EARS
Lugs, Collie-Dugs.

NOSE
Neb, Beak, Bugle, Hooter.

MOUTH
Mooth, Geggie, Gob, Cakehole, Yap.

TEETH
Wallies, Cowdenbeath.

CHIN
Pink (gin).

NECK
Thrapple.

SHOULDERS
Shooders.

ARM
Airm.

ARMPIT
Oxter.

ELBOW
Elby, Spanish-Archer.

HANDS
Hauns, Paws, Mitts.

FINGERS
Fing-urs.

PINKIE
Crannie.

CHEST
Chist.

BREASTS
Paps, Diddies, Swingers,
Sookers.

STOMACH
Gut, Kite.

PENIS
Boaby, Nairobi, Nob,
Dobber, Dick, Walloper,
Dokey, Prick, Wullie,
Giggling-Pin.

THE ERECT PENIS
Bonk-On, Stonner, Raker,
Steamer.

SCROTUM
Baw-bag, Sack,
Clackerbag.

TESTICLES
Baws, Haw-Maws,
Stanes, Dusters, Clems,
Nuts, Conkers.

VAGINA
Fanny, Cunt, Muff, Fud,
Growler, Flange,
Hootenanny, Shareen
Nanjiani, Manto, Twat.

BOTTOM
Erse, Hole, Nat King Cole,
Cameron Toll, Dowp,
Erky, Bahookie, Farter,
Jeer, Bahookie, Ring-piece.

LEGS
Pins, Scrambled Eggs.

FOOT
Fit.

TOE
Tae.

17

DICTIONARY

And finally, a few more handy words for the basic user. Use them wisely and try not to get them in the wrong order. For example, if you refer to someone as 'Ye yelly baw'd basturt,' and they not unreasonably take offence, you may need to quickly refer back to the chapters on Health and Paggers.

aboot	about	*barra*	barrow
acroass	across	*basturt*	bastard
aff	off	*baur*	bother
afore	before	*baws*	balls
ah	I	*berr*	bare
ain	own	*bi*	by
aipple	apple	*bile*	boil
alane	alone	*bit*	but
any'hin	anything	*bits*	boots
anywey	anyway	*blaw*	blow
atween	between	*blint*	blind
auld	old	*boatul*	bottle
aw	all	*boatum*	bottom
awready	already	*boax*	box
awright	alright	*breid*	bread
		brek	break
		broat	brought
		broon	brown

cauld	cold	*git*	get
cairpit	carpet	*guid*	good
claes	clothes	*gless*	glass
coont	count	*goat*	got
dae	do	*hame*	home
deid	dead	*hauf*	half
deif	deaf	*haun*	hand
diz	does	*heid*	head
doaktir	doctor	*herr*	hair
doon	down	*hing*	hang
drap	drop	*hink*	think
dug	dog	*hivin*	heaven
		hoaspital	hospital
		hoat	hot
eftir	after	*hoose*	house
eftirnin	afternoon	*hud*	had
eh	he	*hud*	hold
eh's	his	*huv*	have
erse	arse		
		is	as
fae	from	*it*	at
faimly	family	*ivir*	ever
faw	fall		
fella	fellow	*jaikit*	jacket
ferr	fare	*jist*	just
firiver	forever	*joab*	job
fit	foot		
fitba	football	*kin*	can
flair	floor	*ken*	know
flooers	flowers		
folly	follow	*lang*	long
fun	find	*lit*	let
fur	for	*loast*	lost
furgoat	forgot		
		ma	my
gairdin	garden	*maist*	most
gaun	going	*masel*	myself
gie	give	*membur*	remember
gein	giving	*merrit*	married
gemme	game		

mibbe	maybe		*stert*	start
moose	mouse		*stoap*	stop
n'	and		*tae*	to
nixt	next		*tae*	toe
noo	now		*tap*	top
			telt	told
o'	of		*thair*	their
oaf	off		*thair*	there
oaffice	office		*th'day*	today
oan	on		*thit*	that
oor	our		*thoat*	thought
oot	out		*thum*	them
ower	over		*toap*	top
			toon	town
pairty	party			
perr	pair		*um*	him
perr	poor		*unner*	under
pillie	pillow		*unnerstaun*	understand
pish	piss		*ur*	are
pit	put		*'ur*	her
poakit	pocket		*wan*	one
polis	police		*weel*	well
			wey	way
rid	red		*whae*	who
roond	round		*whair*	where
roondaboot	roundabout		*whin*	when
			whit	what
sair	sore		*wi*	with
seek	sick		*windae*	window
shite	shit		*wiz*	was
shoap	shop		*wull*	will
shurt	shirt		*wursells*	ourselves
soaks	socks			
soajir	soldier		*ye*	you
soond	sound		*yelly*	yellow
sperr	spare		*yersel*	yourself
staun	stand		*yin*	one
sterrs	stairs		*yisturday*	yesterday